DRIVING QUESTIONS & ANSWERS

Over 200 Questions & Answers

by

Jennifer D. Robbins
D.S.A. A.D.I. M.I.A.M. Dip. D.I.

and

Peter W. Robbins
D.S.A. A.D.I. M.I.A.M. Dip. D.I. H.G.V.I.
DIAmond Advanced Instructor

Published by

SHAW & SONS LTD.
Shaway House, Crayford, Kent DA1 4BZ

First Edition 1986
Revised Reprint 1987
Second Edition 1990
Revised Reprint 1991
Revised Reprint 1993

ISBN 0 7219 1045 9

© SHAW & SONS LTD

Printed in Great Britain

CONTENTS

	Page
Introduction	**4**
About the test	4
How to use the booklet	5
Wording of the questions	5
Reasons for failing the oral part of the test	6
Choosing your driving instructor	6
Qualified driving tuition	6
Trainee driving instructors	7
Additional qualifications	7
Questions and answers	**8**
Driving Instructors' Association	**80**
Books by the same authors	**81**

INTRODUCTION

'DRIVING TEST QUESTIONS AND ANSWERS' was written for learner drivers who complained that other books about driving were too complicated. The authors based the questions on those asked most frequently by Department of Transport Driving Standards Agency (D.S.A.) Examiners during actual driving tests. Candidates can check their knowledge of the Highway Code by answering the questions which appear on the left hand pages, and valuable information on other motoring matters is included.

'DRIVING TEST QUESTIONS AND ANSWERS' should be studied in conjunction with 'HOW TO PASS YOUR DRIVING TEST', another book in the popular Robbins series which contains all the information learner drivers want to know.

Learner drivers who follow the advice in these books should not have difficulty passing a driving test the first time. Learners who have failed a previous test can use these publications to identify serious faults, and pass the test at the next attempt.

Candidates must read the Highway Code which will be sent, providing the section requesting a Highway Code booklet is ticked on the driving licence application form.

About the test

Examiners wait until the end of the practical part of the driving test to ask questions about the Highway Code and other motoring matters. Questioning during the driving part of the test would distract a driver. Several questions must be answered correctly, and pictures of road signs are shown to the candidate who is expected to identify them. The examiner tests the candidate's knowledge of other motoring matters such as the legal requirements of tyres, and the causes of skidding. The examiner may give no indication whether the answers are right or wrong. Don't let this worry you.

How to use the booklet

The examiner is appointed by the D.S.A. Many test candidates are frightened at the thought of a stranger watching their driving, and of the practical part of the test. Imagine being in the car with the examiner, and try to create a similar situation by sitting next to a member of your family, or in front of a mirror if you are alone. To prepare for the oral part of the test practise answering a page of questions out loud before checking the answers. Readers who answer questions hesitantly should re-read the relevant information in the Highway Code.

Wording of the questions

Candidates may worry about being nervous on the day of the driving test, and if you do not understand any of the questions ask the examiner to phrase them differently. Avoid quoting long passages of the Highway Code. Use your own words and common sense. If the examiner asks a difficult question don't panic. Think for a moment before answering. Learner drivers practise for the driving part of the driving test, and it makes sense to practise answering questions for the oral part.

Reasons for failing the oral part of the test

Lack of knowledge of the Highway Code is the reason for failing this part of the test. Study the Highway Code before you start driving. Candidates rarely fail under the Highway Code section alone. A knowledge of the code must be demonstrated during the practical part of the driving test, and a learner driver who is unable to answer the questions correctly will display this lack of knowledge during the driving part of the test. A professional driving instructor ensures pupils have a good understanding of the Highway Code.

Choosing your driving instructor

One way is by recommendation, and the Driving Instructors' Association is pleased to give details of qualified instructors, male and female, in your area who comply with high standards and a Code of Practice. As in other professions standards vary widely. A good instructor provides structured tuition in a patient and professional manner, and is proud of producing skilful drivers who pass the driving test first time.

Qualified driving tuition

Any person giving tuition in return for payment, even petrol money, must by law display a valid Approved Driving Instructor (A.D.I.) licence. These are issued by the Driving Standards Agency, an executive agency of the Department of Transport whose motto is 'Safe driving for life.' Qualified instructors have passed examinations testing their driving and teaching ability, and undergo check tests periodically to ensure high standards are maintained. During tuition the green licence, which contains a photograph of the Approved Driving Instructor, must be displayed on the windscreen of the vehicle being used.

Trainee driving instructors

Trainee instructors, who have not passed the examination which tests instructional ability must display a pink licence, and this is issued for a period of six months only. A learner driver should check a licence is being displayed before paying for tuition, and state if tuition from a fully qualified instructor is required. If an A.D.I. licence or trainee licence is not on show during lessons, ask why.

Additional qualifications

There is an additional qualification, the Diploma of Driving Instruction awarded jointly by the Associated Examining Board and the Driving Instructors' Association. Only a small percentage of instructors hold this coveted diploma and have passed five sets of examinations testing driving theory, skills and procedures; instructing practice and techniques; vehicle maintenance and mechanical principles; legal obligations and regulations; and management of a driving school.

A number of diploma holders have also passed the Department of Transport's Special Cardington driving test at 'A' level, and qualified as DIAmond Advanced Instructors.

QUESTIONS

Driving test questions and answers

1. How much room should a driver leave when passing a parked vehicle?

2. What do these warning signs mean?

   (a)    (b)

3. How much alcohol can a driver drink and be fit to drive?

4. When is it safe to beckon a pedestrian to cross the road?

5. What does this sign mean?

ANSWERS

1. Enough room for a door to open or a child to run into the road.

---

2. (a) Two-way traffic straight ahead.
   (b) Two-way traffic crosses one way road.
   (Red bordered triangles, black arrows)

---

3. The risk of an accident increases sharply beyond the legal limit of 35 microgrammes of alcohol per 100 millilitres of breath. Inexperienced drivers or those who drink infrequently can be impaired BELOW this limit. **DO NOT DRINK AND DRIVE.**

---

4. **Never.** Allow others to make their own judgement of whether it is safe to cross. A pedestrian could be beckoned into the path of another vehicle.

---

5. End of temporary restriction on a motorway.

QUESTIONS

6. How does a driver know when an indicator bulb has failed?

---

7. What precautions should be taken before leaving a car parked on a slope?

---

8. What do these signs mean?

    (a)    (b)

---

9. Could a test candidate fail on the Highway Code part of the driving test only?

---

10. Why is it important to keep a vehicle clean in the winter?

---

11. Which lane should be used when driving at 70mph on a three lane motorway?

ANSWERS

6. The audible flashing warning light on the dashboard flashes faster.

---

7. Apply the handbrake. Leave the car in a forward gear when parking facing uphill, and reverse gear when facing downhill. Turn the wheels into the kerb.

---

8. (a) Holiday route (yellow sign, black lettering).
   (b) Ring road.

---

9. It is possible but unlikely. A driver who does not know the Highway Code will fail the oral part of the driving test, and also the practical part as safe driving is dependent on a good knowledge of the Highway Code.

---

10. Lights and windows become obscured with dirt and spray. Salt on roads can corrode and damage the bodywork including tyres.

---

11. Drive in the left hand lane unless overtaking or directed otherwise by signs.

QUESTIONS

12. What do these signs mean?

(a) 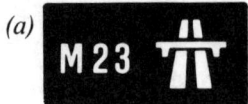 (b)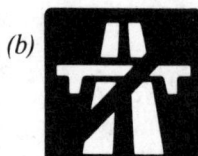

---

13. Explain the TWO SECOND RULE.

---

14. What do these warning signs mean?

(a) 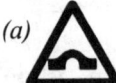 (b)

---

15. How are stopping distances affected by wet weather?

---

16. What would you do if you missed your motorway exit?

12

ANSWERS

12. (a) Start of motorway (blue background, white lettering).
    (b) End of motorway (blue background, white lettering, red diagonal line).

---

13. Leave a two second safety gap between your vehicle and the vehicle in front. Measure two seconds by repeating the phrase, 'Only a fool breaks the two second rule.' This takes two seconds to say.

---

14. (a) Hump bridge ahead (red border).
    (b) Uneven road surface (red border).

---

15. Stopping distances are doubled in wet weather. Apply the brakes more gently to avoid the wheels locking and causing a skid.

---

16. Leave by the next exit. NEVER REVERSE OR DO A U-TURN. Study a recent map before a journey, and note down junction exit numbers.

QUESTIONS

17. What should you do if dazzled by the headlights of an oncoming vehicle?

---

18. Explain these warning signs.

  (a)    (b)

---

19. On which side of the road are warning posts with red reflectors?

---

20. What is the overall stopping distance of a car travelling at 60mph in good conditions?

---

21. What must a driver NOT do on the yellow criss-cross lines of a box junction?

---

22. What warning does this sign give?

ANSWERS

17. Slow down. Stop if necessary. Never flash headlights in return or other drivers may be blinded with tragic results.

---

18. (a) Opening or swing bridge ahead (red border).
    (b) Quayside or river bank (red border).

---

19. Posts with red reflectors are on the left.

---

20. 73 metres (240ft). The answer of one metre for each mph would be acceptable.

---

21. A driver must not stop on the box unless waiting for oncoming traffic to pass before turning right.

---

22. Sharp deviation of route to left.

QUESTIONS

23. What are the legal requirements for tyres?

24. Is it legal to mix radial and cross ply tyres on the same vehicle?

25. How would a driver leave a motorway to visit a town on the right hand side of the carriageway?

26. What does this sign mean?

27. What action should a driver take if an accident occurs ahead?

28. Describe how to drive through flood water safely.

ANSWERS

23. Tyres must not have bald patches, cuts, splits, or other defects. Tread depth should be at least 1.6 millimetres, and the tyres should be inflated to the pressure recommended by the manufacturer of the vehicle.

---

24. Radial and cross ply tyres must NEVER be mixed on the SAME AXLE. When radial and cross ply tyres are on the same vehicle, the radial tyres must be on the rear axle or an offence is committed.

---

25. By a sliproad on the left. There are no right turns on a motorway.

---

26. National speed limit applies; 70mph on motorways and dual carriageways, and 60mph on other roads unless otherwise indicated.

---

27. Stop in a safe place. Warn other traffic.

---

28. Drive through the shallowest part in first gear slowly and keeping the engine speed high. Maintain a low speed by slipping the clutch. Avoid making waves.

QUESTIONS

29. What does a flashing amber light signify?

---

30. What do these signs mean (blue backgrounds)?

(a)  *(b)*

---

31. Describe what these warning signs mean.

(a) 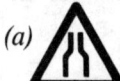 *(b)*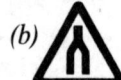

---

32. What actions are illegal within the zig zag lines of a pedestrian crossing?

---

33. What rules apply to parking in fog?

---

34. When should dim dip lights be used?

ANSWERS

29. A slow moving vehicle ahead such as a tractor; or a vehicle that has broken down.

---

30. (a) Trams only.
    (b) Pedestrian crossing point over tramway.

---

31. (a) Road narrows on both sides (red border).
    (b) Dual carriageway ends (red border).

---

32. Drivers must not park or overtake the leading vehicle within the zig zag lines on the approach to a crossing. Even when there are no zig zags do not overtake. Pedestrians have right of way.

---

33. It is dangerous to park on the road in fog. When there is nowhere else to park, leave the sidelights on.

---

34. In dull weather or when there is good street lighting at night.

QUESTIONS

35. When must a driver stop at a pedestrian crossing?

36. What should you do before leaving a vehicle?

37. What do flashing amber lights on motorway signs mean?

38. Can any driver supervise a learner driver?

39. How many mirrors are required by law on a private car?

40. Identify these signs.

   (a)    (b)

41. What direction should a parked vehicle face at night?

ANSWERS

35. When pedestrians are on the crossing.

---

36. Switch off the engine and headlights. Apply the handbrake and remove the key. Check the windows are closed and remove anything valuable and lock the vehicle.

---

37. Flashing amber lights warn of a hazard ahead, such as right lane closed. Reduce speed to below 30mph.

---

38. A supervising driver must be at least 21 years old, and have held a full driving licence for three years.

---

39. Two mirrors, one mounted internally.

---

40. (a) Stop and give way sign.
    (b) Give way to traffic on major road (red border).

---

41. The same way as the traffic flow.

QUESTIONS

42. When can hazard warning lights be used on a moving vehicle?

---

43. What action should a driver take if a car begins to skid during braking?

---

44. What do the following warning signs mean?

(a)  (b)

---

45. What documents are needed to drive a vehicle?

---

46. Why is extra care needed when turning right nearside to nearside?

---

47. Explain the meaning of amber flashing lights at a pelican crossing.

---

48. What would you do if the word 'fog' appeared on a road sign and the road appeared to be clear?

ANSWERS

42. On a motorway or dual carriageway where the national speed limit applies if there is a hazard ahead.

43. Release the brake pedal.

44. (a) Double bend, first to the left (may be reversed) (red border).
    (b) Road narrows on right (left if reversed) (red border).

45. Vehicle licence (tax disc), motor insurance, driving licence, MoT certificate if applicable, and registration documents.

46. An approaching vehicle turning right can obstruct your view of oncoming traffic.

47. Drivers must give way to pedestrians on the crossing when the flashing amber lights show, but may drive on when the crossing is clear.

48. Be prepared for drifting fog which can occur in patches.

QUESTIONS

49. What do the following signs mean?

    (a) 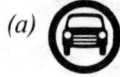   (b)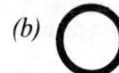

---

50. How would police in a police car signal a driver to pull over?

---

51. What is the 'Rule of the Road'?

---

52. When should a driver use rear fog lamps?

---

53. What do the following signs mean?

    (a)    (b)

---

54. What are the rules for driving in snow?

ANSWERS

49. (a) No motor vehicles except solo motorcycles, scooters or mopeds (red border).
    (b) No vehicles (red border).

---

50. The police car headlights or blue light will flash. The siren or horn may be sounded. A police officer will point and use the left indicator.

---

51. Drive on the left unless overtaking, turning right or otherwise directed by road signs, markings or traffic controllers.

---

52. Rear fog lamps should not be switched on unless visibility is reduced below 100 metres, otherwise they will dazzle following traffic.

---

53. (a) No vehicles including load over weight shown (in tonnes) (red border).
    (b) No goods vehicles over maximum gross weight shown (in tonnes) (red border).

---

54. Do not go out unless the journey is essential. Drive slowly in as high a gear as possible to avoid wheel spin. Avoid harsh (ABC) acceleration, braking and cornering. Switch on headlights in falling snow.

QUESTIONS

55. What does it mean when a traffic controller facing you raises his/her right arm?

56. What would you do if your vehicle broke down on a level crossing?

57. Who would carry a white stick with two reflective bands?

58. What do the following signs forbid?

   (a)    (b)

59. Where are drivers allowed to stop and park on a motorway, for example if very tired?

60. In what order do the traffic lights change, starting with red?

ANSWERS

55. You must stop.

---

56. Get passengers out and to a place of safety. Use the telephone to inform the signalman. IF SAFE try to push the vehicle clear, BUT take care and keep clear if the alarm rings or lights flash.

---

57. A deaf and blind person.

---

58. (a) No cycling (red border).
    (b) No vehicles over 12 seats except regular scheduled school and works buses (red border).

---

59. Drivers are only allowed to park at the service areas of the motorway. It is extremely dangerous to stop on the hard shoulder, which is for emergencies only.

---

60. RED; RED AND AMBER; GREEN; AMBER; RED.

QUESTIONS

61. Explain the meaning of each traffic light.

---

62. What must you NOT do where you see the following signs?

(a)   (b)

---

63. What is the ideal separation distance to leave between yourself and other traffic on a dry day when travelling at 20mph?

---

64. What do red or amber lights indicate at a level crossing?

---

65. When should drivers drive with dipped headlights during the day time?

---

66. What does the following sign tell drivers they must do?

28

ANSWERS

61. They all mean stop except green which allows drivers to drive on IF the way is clear. Drivers may continue if the amber light appears only after they have crossed the line or are so close to it that to pull up might cause an accident.

62. (a) Turn Left (No left turn) (red border).
    (b) Make a U turn (No U turn) (red border).

63. 12 metres (40feet) overall stopping distance.
    [6 metres (20 feet) thinking distance plus
    6 metres (20 feet) braking distance.]

64. Both lights mean STOP, a train is approaching. If the lights continue to show after the train has passed, drivers must wait as another train may be approaching.

65. Dipped headlights must be used during poor visibility, fog, snow, mist, or heavy rain.

66. Give priority to vehicles from opposite direction (red border and small red arrow).

QUESTIONS

67. What does a flashing green light signify?

68. What is the correct course of action if a car breaks down on a motorway?

69. What effect would overloading the rear of a car have on the headlights?

70. What do these signs warn drivers?

(a)    *(b)*

ANSWERS

67. Doctor on an emergency call. Give way as soon as possible.

---

68. Stop on the hard shoulder as far from the carriageway as possible.
Switch on hazard warning lights.
Passengers should exit from doors on the nearside of the vehicle (away from the carriageway), and wait well back from the motorway with children kept under strict control. People sitting in the car are at risk from a collision with another vehicle. Animals must be left in the car for road safety reasons.
Place a warning triangle 150 metres behind the car.
Ring for assistance from the nearest emergency telephone. These are indicated by marker posts.
NEVER cross the carriageway.
Women travelling alone are advised to get into the car and lock the doors if another motorist stops.

---

69. The headlights would need realigning to avoid dazzling oncoming drivers.

---

70. (a) Children going to or from school or playground (red border).
    (b) Slippery road (red border).

QUESTIONS

71. What is the overall stopping distance of a car travelling at 30mph in good conditions?

72. When is it illegal for a driver to sound the horn of a vehicle?

73. What do these signs mean (red circles)?

   (a) 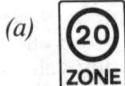   (b)

74. What does the following sign mean, and where might you see it?

75. What should a driver not do when being overtaken?

76. What do these signs mean?

   (a)

   Red triangle

   (b)   Yellow sign, black border/figures (displayed in front or rear window of bus or coach)

ANSWERS

71. 23 metres (75 feet).

---

72. Between 11.30 pm and 7.00 am (2330-0700) in a built-up area, or when the vehicle is stopped, unless in danger from a moving vehicle.

---

73. (a) Entry to 20mph zone.
    (b) End of 20mph zone.

---

74. Vehicles may pass either side to reach the same destination. This sign is used in one way streets (blue background, white arrows).

---

75. Drivers should not increase speed. Allow the overtaking vehicle to pass safely.

---

76. (a) Trams crossing ahead.
    (b) School bus.

QUESTIONS

77. Describe how to apply and release the steering lock on a car.

---

78. What do the following signs mean?

    (a)    (b)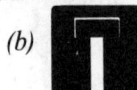

---

79. When may a driver drive on after the traffic lights have changed to amber?

---

80. On which side of the road are warning posts with amber reflectors?

---

81. What action can a driver take when the vehicle behind is following too closely?

ANSWERS

77. After switching off the engine turn the steering wheel until the lock is applied and the steering wheel will not turn. To release the lock, insert the key and, while turning it, try to turn the steering wheel until the lock is released. The steering lock is a deterrent to car thieves.

78. (a) No pedestrians (red border).
    (b) No through road (blue background, red and white T).

79. A driver may drive on if the vehicle has already crossed the STOP line when the amber light shows, or if it is unsafe to stop.

80. Posts with amber reflectors are on the right hand side of the road.

81. Slow down gradually and safely to allow the vehicle to pass. Never brake sharply to frighten the following driver. This could cause an accident.

QUESTIONS

82. Where is it illegal to park?

---

83. Identify the following signs.

    (a)    (b)

---

84. Why should care be taken before opening a car door?

---

85. What are motorway acceleration lanes for?

---

86. Where are the red coloured studs on motorways and dual carriageways?

---

87. What do the following signs prohibit?

    (a)   (b)

ANSWERS

82. On motorways; within zig zag lines at a pedestrian crossing; on clearways; where there are solid white lines in the centre of the road; in a bus or cycle lane when operative; near to a road junction; facing oncoming traffic at night; and where parking restrictions apply.

---

83. (a) Roundabout (red border).
    (b) Mini-roundabout (blue background, white arrows).

---

84. It is an offence to open your car door and endanger other road users.

---

85. An acceleration lane allows a motorist to adjust the speed of a vehicle to join the motorway traffic in a suitable gap.

---

86. Red studs are on the left hand side of the carriageway.

---

87. (a) No vehicle or combination of vehicles over length shown (red border).
    (b) No vehicles over height shown (red border).

QUESTIONS

88. How far apart are the blue count down markers to motorway exits?

89. Name three situations when a driver MUST NOT reverse?

90. Why is it necessary to check tyre pressures regularly?

91. What do the following signs prohibit?

　　(a)　　　　　　　*(b)*

ANSWERS

88. They are placed 100 yards apart at distances of 300, 200, and 100 yards from the motorway exit.

89. On motorways.
    Out of a side road into a main road.
    For longer than necessary.

90. It is an offence to have improperly inflated tyres, and a loss of pressure can be an indication of a defect in the tyre. Check pressures weekly. The recommended pressure is printed in the manufacturer's handbook. Take care not to confuse metric and imperial measurements on the gauge as this can result in accidents and is dangerous.

91. (a) No motor vehicles (red border).
    (b) No overtaking (red border, black and red cars).

QUESTIONS

92. Are arm signals useful when a car has indicators?

---

93. Demonstrate a slowing down arm signal.

---

94. Demonstrate a turning left arm signal.

---

95. What are the following warning signs?

(a) ⚠️ (b) ⚠️

---

96. State three instances when it is an offence to overtake another vehicle.

ANSWERS

92. Yes. A slowing down signal can alert pedestrians waiting to cross at a crossing that a driver intends to slow and stop. A right turn signal can confirm an impending right turn after passing a parked vehicle.

---

93. Fully extend the right arm and move it up and down a few times. Hold the wheel with both hands when stopping.

---

94. Fully extend the right arm and move it in a circle anti-clockwise.

---

95. (a) T junction (red border).
    (b) Staggered junction (red border).

---

96. When there are double white lines in the centre of the road drivers must not cross a solid line on their side.
    In the zig zag lines approaching a pedestrian crossing.
    When there is a **NO OVERTAKING** sign.

QUESTIONS

97. What are the rules for driving where there are tram ways?

---

98. How much clearance should a driver leave when overtaking a cyclist?

---

99. Identify the following warning signs.

(a) ⚠️ 10%   *(b)* ⚠️ 20%

---

100. Which vehicles are not allowed to use the third, right hand, lane on a motorway?

---

101. Which lane should be used for turning right out of a one way street?

---

102. Name the parts of the car which must be properly maintained.

ANSWERS

97.
- ★ Do not enter a road or lane reserved for trams.
- ★ Diamond shaped signs are for tram drivers only.
- ★ Watch out for areas used by trams. Do not park there.
- ★ Give way to trams and do not race or overtake them.

98. Leave enough space that should a cyclist wobble, swerve, or fall, a collision would not occur.

99. (a) Steep hill downwards (red border).
    (b) Steep hill upwards (red border).

100. Heavy goods vehicles over 7.5 tonnes.
Buses longer than 12 metres (40 feet).
Vehicles towing caravans or trailers.

101. The right hand lane.

102. It is an offence not to maintain: the brakes, steering, tyres, windscreen wipers and washers, seat belts, mirrors, horn, speedometer, exhaust system, lights, reflectors, indicators. Loads must be secure.

QUESTIONS

103. What is the significance of END OF DUAL CARRIAGEWAY signs?

---

104. What do the following warning signs inform drivers?
(a)   (b)

---

105. Name three groups of people with the authority to direct traffic.

---

106. When does a bus have priority?

---

107. How far behind a vehicle should a warning triangle be placed;
(a) on a road with two way traffic?
(b) on a motorway?

---

108. What do red triangular road signs mean?

---

109. What do the following road signs mean?
(a)   (b)

ANSWERS

103. Drivers must adapt to two way traffic or a collision could occur.

---

104. (a) Change to opposite carriageway (red border).
     (b) Traffic merges from left with equal priority (red border).

---

105. The police; traffic wardens; school crossing patrols with a STOP-CHILDREN sign.

---

106. Drivers should give way to coaches and buses signalling an intention to move out from bus stops.

---

107. (a) 50 metres on a road with two way traffic.
     (b) 150 metres on motorways.

---

108. Triangular signs are warning signs.

---

109. (a) Danger (plate specifies nature of danger) (red border).
     (b) Wild animals (red border).

QUESTIONS

110. Who is responsible for passengers wearing seat belts?

111. What is the right-hand lane for on a two-lane dual carriageway?

112. What do green traffic lights mean?

113. Identify the following road signs.

(a) *(b)*

114. What are the safety rules for car telephones?

115. What precautions are needed after driving through flood water?

116. How can a driver dry the brakes after driving through flood water?

ANSWERS

110. The driver is responsible for him/herself and children in the vehicle. Adult passengers are responsible for themselves.

---

111. Overtaking or turning right.

---

112. Green traffic lights mean GO IF CLEAR. Anticipate a green light might change on approach, and check both ways before driving on at crossroads.

---

113. (a) Level crossing with barrier or gate ahead (red border).
     (b) Level crossing without barrier or gate ahead (red border).

---

114. Do not hold a telephone when driving. Find a safe place to stop before using. Do not allow a hands-free microphone to distract you.

---

115. The brakes may not work properly when wet, and should be tested.

---

116. After checking in the mirrors that it is safe, drive slowly with the left foot resting lightly on the brake pedal.

QUESTIONS

117. How long would it take to stop a vehicle travelling at 50mph?

118. Explain the following signs.

(a) (b)

119. What does this road marking mean?

120. What should a driver switch on in fog?

121. Name three causes of skidding.

48

ANSWERS

117. 53 metres (175 feet).

---

118. (a) Traffic signals (red border, red, amber, and green light).
     (b) Warning, cyclists (red border).

---

119. When the line nearest the vehicle is broken a driver may cross the line when it is safe to do so. Parking is not allowed.

---

120. Dipped headlights; windscreen wipers; fog lights.

---

121. Remember A.B.C.
     Harsh Acceleration.
     Harsh Braking.
     Harsh Cornering.

QUESTIONS

122. What do the following warning signs mean?

(a)   (b)

123. When is overtaking on the left allowed?

124. What do red flashing lights in the central reservation or a slip road mean?

125. List the four actions that enable an emergency stop to be made safely.

126. What does the following sign mean?

ANSWERS

122. (a) Loose chippings (red border).
     (b) Low flying aircraft or sudden noise (red border).

---

123. When traffic is turning right.
     Where a filter system is in operation.
     In a one way street.
     When traffic is moving slowly in queues.

---

124. You must not go beyond the signal in any lane.

---

125. Hold the wheel firmly in both hands.
     Brake firmly but progressively without locking the wheels.
     To aid braking, leave the clutch alone until the vehicle is almost stationary.
     Do not apply the handbrake until the vehicle has stopped.

---

126. Priority over vehicles from opposite direction (blue background, white and red arrows).

QUESTIONS

127. What should a driver do after stopping in a safe place when an accident has occurred ahead?

128. Falling asleep at the wheel is a cause of accidents. If you feel sleepy while driving on a motorway what should you do?

129. What action should be taken to correct a rear wheel skid?

130. What do the following road markings mean?

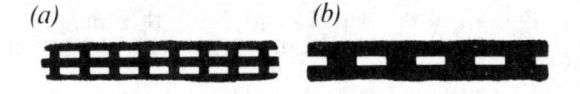

(a) *(b)*

131. How often should drivers have their eyesight checked?

132. What would be the overall stopping distance of a car travelling at 40mph in wet conditions?

ANSWERS

127. Warn other traffic to prevent further danger. Switch on hazard lights.

---

128. Do not stop on the hard shoulder. Open a window for fresh air, and stop at the next service area to rest. Do not drive when tired.

---

129. Turn into the skid but beware of over correction.

---

130. (a) Give way to traffic on major road.
     (b) Give way to traffic from right at roundabout.

---

131. Every two years unless recommended otherwise. One of the requirements for holders of a driving licence is the ability to read a number plate at 20.5 metres (about 67 feet). Regular eye tests will ensure prompt treatment of glaucoma and other potentially serious conditions.

---

132. 73 metres (240 feet) which is DOUBLE the normal stopping distance of 36 metres.

QUESTIONS

133. What precaution should be taken before driving past stationary buses, coaches, ice cream vans, or vehicles offering goods for sale?

---

134. What do these signs mean?

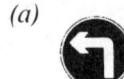

(a) *(b)* *(c)*

---

135. What would cause the ignition (battery) warning light to flash when the car was being driven?

---

136. Why is it sometimes useful to change down a gear before overtaking?

---

137. What precautions should a driver take before starting the engine?

---

138. Why is it dangerous to follow the tail lights of a vehicle in fog or snow?

ANSWERS

133. Slow down and anticipate that someone, especially a child, may run out from behind a parked vehicle. "I didn't have a chance to stop," is a familiar defence from drivers after such accidents, and anticipation is vital.

---

134. (a) Turn left ahead (blue background, white arrow).
 (b) Turn left (blue background, white arrow).
 (c) Keep left (blue background, white arrow).

---

135. Generator failure or the fan belt not functioning.

---

136. The lower the gear the more power to accelerate, and speed can be increased more quickly.

---

137. Check the handbrake is on, and the gears are in neutral.

---

138. The tail lights of the vehicle in front may disappear from view if the fog becomes thicker. Trying to 'catch' the vehicle could result in a collision.

QUESTIONS

139. What must you do in the event of breakdown on a motorway if you are unable to get your vehicle to the hard shoulder?

140. State the routine all drivers should follow before any driving action involving a change in position or speed.

141. If the vehicle ahead has an accident and is carrying a hazardous load, what is the correct course of action?

142. What should a driver do if amber lights flash and alarm bells ring when driving across a level crossing?

143. What parking rules apply in a 30mph or less speed limit?

ANSWERS

139. ★ Switch on hazard warning lights.
 ★ Stay in the vehicle if you cannot get clear of the carriageway safely.
 ★ Do not put a warning triangle on the carriageway.

---

140. MIRRORS SIGNAL MANOEUVRE. Check the mirrors thoroughly and then signal if necessary before any manoeuvre.

---

141. Stay well back from the vehicle, and alert the emergency services. Full protective clothing may have to be worn and the emergency services are trained to deal with such situations. Vehicles carrying hazardous loads must display a hazard information panel with a diamond sign indicating the risk; for example:
 (a) Flammable substance sign.
 (b) Corrosive substance sign.

---

142. Do not stop on the crossing. If the vehicle is already on the crossing keep going.

---

143. Lights are not needed if the vehicle is parked:
 ★ 10 metres from a junction.
 ★ Close to the kerb in a place where parking is allowed.
 ★ Facing the same way as the traffic flow.

QUESTIONS

144. List five driving actions before which a driver must check in the mirrors.

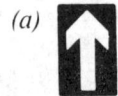

---

145. What do the following signs mean?

(a) *(b)*

---

146. Where must a driver stop at a pedestrian crossing?

---

147. What would be the most likely cause of no current when the ignition key was turned?

---

148. Why should a driver pay special attention to speed when leaving a motorway?

148a. What do these symbols mean (yellow background)?

ANSWERS

144. Before signalling.
 Before changing direction.
 Before overtaking.
 Before slowing.
 Before stopping.

---

145. (a) One way traffic (blue background, white arrow).
 (b) Ahead only (blue background, white arrow).

---

146. Drivers must stop at the give way line one metre from the crossing.

---

147. Battery leads loose or disconnected.

---

148. Many motorway exits have sharp bends joining non-motorway roads. Drivers must adjust and reduce speed.

148a. They show emergency diversion routes for motorway traffic.

QUESTIONS

149. What do white striped hazard lines mean?

---

150. Which vehicles are not allowed to use motorways?

---

151. Which drivers are not allowed to use motorways?

---

152. List the three actions of a manoeuvre in the order they occur.

---

153. What rules should be followed regarding the barriers at an automatic half barrier level crossing?

ANSWERS

149. Do not drive over these areas unless unavoidable. The hazard lines prevent collisions, especially when drivers are turning right. Do not enter where the chevrons have a solid edged white line.

---

150. Tractors, slow moving vehicles, low power motorcycles or mopeds, bicycles, and some invalid carriages.

---

151. Learner drivers.

---

152. POSITION the vehicle correctly.
SPEED slow if necessary.
LOOK all round.

---

153. Drivers must never zig zag round the barriers or an accident could occur. Wait for the barriers to be lifted before attempting to cross the crossing.

QUESTIONS

154. What is the safe course of action if the flashing blue lights of an emergency vehicle appear in the rear view mirror?

155. What do the following signs mean?

(a) (b)

156. What rules should drivers observe regarding bus lanes?

157. By how much does the stopping distance of a vehicle increase during icy weather?

158. What should a driver do if a suitcase falls from the roof rack on to the motorway?

159. What does the following sign mean (blue background, red cross and border)?

ANSWERS

154. Drivers should move their vehicles out of the way as soon as it is safe for the emergency vehicle to pass. Never stop suddenly.

---

155. (a) With-flow bus lane (blue background, white markings).
    (b) Contra-flow bus lane (blue background, white markings).

---

156. Keep out of the bus lanes during the times stated.

---

157. The stopping distance will increase by at least TEN times the normal stopping distance. Drive slowly and allow extra separation distance between vehicles.

---

158. Stop on the hard shoulder and ring from the nearest emergency telephone for assistance. NEVER retrieve a fallen load from a motorway.

---

159. A clearway sign means a driver may not stop or park a vehicle on the carriageway.

QUESTIONS

160. What final check should a driver make before reversing, and why?

161. How long would it take for a driver to react to an emergency when travelling at 30mph?

162. How should a driver signal and position a vehicle when turning right at a roundabout?

163. What do blue circular signs mean?

164. What traffic has priority at a roundabout?

165. When should a driver use main beam headlights?

ANSWERS

160. Look all round and behind the car. Children may not be seen when playing behind a vehicle.

161. The thinking distance would be 9 metres (30 feet). The overall stopping distance would be 23 metres (75 feet).

162. Signal right on approach and move into the right hand lane. When past the exit before the one being taken, signal left to exit. When safe move into the left hand lane to leave the roundabout, and if this lane is obstructed leave in the right hand lane.

163. They are mostly mandatory — things a driver must do.

164. Drivers must give way to traffic approaching from the immediate right.

165. At night on unlit roads when there is no oncoming traffic or vehicles travelling ahead.

QUESTIONS

166. When would a driver use this arm signal? (I want to go straight on.)

---

167. What separation distance should be left between vehicles travelling at 70mph?

---

168. When is it illegal for a driver to drive?

---

169. How will the examiner test a candidate's knowledge of road signs during a driving test?

---

170. If a candidate disagrees with the decision of an examiner at the end of a driving test, can the decision be changed?

170a. Alternately flashing red lights mean you must stop your vehicle. Where would you see them?

ANSWERS

166. To let a policeman know the intention is to go straight ahead at a crossroads.

167. 96 metres (315 feet). The answer of one metre for each mph would be acceptable.

168. Drivers must not drive if their driving would be impaired by drugs, drink, illness, or poor vision.

169. The examiner will ask the candidate to identify pictures of road signs.

170. The examiner's decision is final since the examiner knows how the test candidate drove, and only the examiner has the authority to pass or fail the candidate. When a test is not conducted properly a learner may appeal for a new test to be awarded free of charge.

170a. At level crossings, lifting bridges, airfields, fire stations, etc.

QUESTIONS

171. What do these parking restrictions mean?

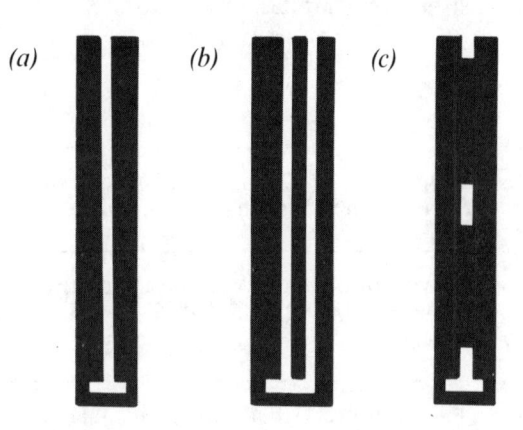

(a) *(b)* *(c)*

172. What should a driver do in the event of a burst tyre while driving?

173. What parts of the vehicle is it essential to keep clean?

174. What rules apply at a pedestrian crossing with an island in the middle?

ANSWERS

171. (a) No parking during working hours (solid yellow line).
    (b) No parking for most or all of the time (two solid yellow lines).
    (c) Parking restricted to short periods (broken yellow lines).
    Look at the time plates for the exact restriction in force.

172. Hold the wheel firmly and use the brakes as little as possible to minimise the risk of swerving. Aim to allow the car to roll to a halt safely.

173. The windscreen, windows, lights, indicators, mirrors, and reflectors.

174. A pedestrian crossing with an island in the middle should be treated as two separate crossings.

QUESTIONS

175. How far apart are the emergency telephones on a motorway?

176. Who has priority on a hill?

177. What do these signs mean?

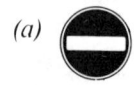

    (a)   *(b)*

178. Why should casualties in a road accident not be moved?

179. When should headlights be turned on at the end of the day?

180. What is the middle lane on a three-lane road for?

181. What do the following signs mean?

    (a) ▶7·6◀   *(b)* 2T

ANSWERS

175. At one mile intervals.

---

176. Give way to traffic driving UPHILL.

---

177. (a) No entry for vehicular traffic (red background).
(b) Pedestrian crossing (red border).

---

178. Moving casualties increases the likelihood of shock and further injuries. Leave injured people in their cars unless at risk from fire or further collision.

---

179. Switch on headlights at lighting up time, or earlier if visibility is poor. Be the first to use headlights and not the last.

---

180. Where the road markings do not specify priority, use the middle lane for overtaking or turning right. Remember you have no more right to use the middle lane than a driver approaching from the opposite direction.

---

181. (a) No vehicles over width shown (red border).
(b) Axle weight limit in tonnes (red border).

QUESTIONS

182. How soon should the police be notified when an accident causes injury to a person, vehicle, or animal?

---

183. What are the two main dangers at a road traffic accident?

---

184. What lights should a parked vehicle show at night?

---

185. What lane should be used by drivers going straight ahead at a roundabout?

---

186. Where are motorway warning signals situated?

---

187. Identify the following signs.

   (a) **30**   (b) 🚲

ANSWERS

182. If the driver is unable to give details of his or her name and address to the other parties involved, the accident should be reported to the police as soon as possible, and within 24 hours.

---

183. Further collision.
Fire.
Warn other traffic by use of hazard warning lights and other warning signs. Check engines are switched off and cigarettes extinguished.

---

184. NO lights are required on a road subject to a 30mph speed limit. On other roads cars must show side lights, tail lights, and registration plate lights.

---

185. Use the left hand lane whenever possible, unless otherwise indicated by road markings or traffic conditions.

---

186. On the central reservation where they apply to all lanes or overhead as a signal for each lane.

---

187. (a) Minimum speed limit 30mph (blue background, white numbers).
(b) Route to be used by pedal cyclists only (blue background, white bicycle).

QUESTIONS

188. When should the handbrake be used?

---

189. Describe the routine for safe overtaking.

---

190. What should you do if a dog runs in front of your vehicle?

---

191. What do these motorway signs mean?
(a)   *(b)*

---

192. What do signs in a red circle mean?

---

193. What do flashing headlights mean?

ANSWERS

188. The handbrake should be applied at STOP junctions, when the vehicle is stationary for more than a few seconds, and before leaving the vehicle.

---

189. Ask yourself whether the manoeuvre is necessary. Use the POSITION SPEED LOOK routine. Position the car ready for overtaking and check that the speed of your vehicle is adequate to complete the manoeuvre. Look ahead and behind and then use the MIRROR SIGNAL MANOEUVRE ROUTINE. Repeat as necessary.

---

190. Decelerate but do not swerve. Avoid braking sharply if this would endanger others.

---

191. (a) Change lane.
     (b) Leave motorway at next exit.

---

192. They are mostly prohibitive — things a driver MUST NOT DO.

---

193. Headlights should be flashed as a warning only, and care should be taken if another driver is using them as a signal.

QUESTIONS

194. When should a driver use the right hand lane to leave a roundabout?

195. Which drivers are exempt from having to wear a seat belt?

196. What problems are associated with light steering?

197. What would warn a driver of a soft tyre when driving?

198. Where would a driver see amber and green studs on a motorway or dual carriageway?

199. What colours are primary route signs?

200. When may you drive on at a red traffic light?

ANSWERS

194. Drivers should use the right hand lane when the left hand lane is obstructed by slow moving traffic.

---

195. The following situations provide exemption: drivers with a medical certificate; local delivery van drivers, taxi drivers, or those carrying out a manoeuvre which includes reversing.

---

196. Light steering may be a warning of black ice, or a sign the car is beginning to aquaplane on a wet road. Reduce speed.

---

197. Steering feels heavier than usual and will pull to one side.

---

198. Amber studs mark the right hand edge of the carriageway, and green studs mark the acceleration and deceleration lanes.

---

199. White place names and yellow route numbers on a green background.

---

200. When you are going in the direction shown by a green filter arrow and the way is clear.

QUESTIONS

201. Why is it essential for a driver to check behind and alongside before altering direction?

---

202. What do these (yellow) lines on the curb mean?

(a) (b) (c)

ANSWERS

201. Mirrors have blind spots, and drivers should check it is safe before any manoeuvre.

202. Loading restrictions. No loading or unloading at times shown on nearby plates. If no days are indicated on the sign, the restrictions are in force every day including Sundays and Bank Holidays.
    (a) During every working day.
    (b) During every working day, and additional times.
    (c) During any other periods.

DRIVING INSTRUCTORS' ASSOCIATION

Driving Instructors' Association Ltd.
Safety House
Beddington Farm Road
Croydon CR0 4XZ
Telephone 081-665 5151

will be pleased to supply details of highly qualified driving instructors in your area.

Note: Whilst every attempt has been made to ensure the complete accuracy of the answers given in this book, neither the authors nor the publishers can accept liability for any error or misinterpretation resulting from their use.